First published in the United Kingdom in 2014 by
Portico Books
10 Southcombe Street
London
W14 0RA

An imprint of Anova Books Company Ltd

ISBN 978 1 909396 42 5

A CIP catalogue record for this book is available
from the British Library.

10 9 8 7 6 5 4 3 2 1

Printed and bound by Times Offset (M) Sdn Bhd, Malaysia
Illustrations by Damien Weighill

This book can be ordered direct from the publisher at
www.anovabooks.com

The boring bit!

CooL Art

PORTICO

Simon Armstrong

50 faNtaStic Facts FOR KiDs OF aLL Ages

CONTENTS

Welcome to the World of Cool Art!

Art is everywhere. It is in everything. And, for some, it is in nothing. Art can be on TV, and the TV itself can be art. Art can divide us all, and it can unite us all. It can entertain us, it can educate us, and it can reveal new things to us – and it can do all these things at the same time.

William Shakespeare, the world's most famous playwright, once wrote, 'Beauty is bought by judgement of the eye', and he's right. The beauty and brilliance of all the art in the world – from billboard advertisements to self-portraits, and everything in between – lies in the eyes of the beholder. YOU. That's the best thing about art – it is what you make of it.

But, as many art experts and historians believe, in order to pass judgement and scrutiny on art, you must first open your mind to all the types of art that exist, and learn about the amazing history of the various types of art there are from all over the world, how art is created and appreciated, and what it can say about the world around us, even if its intention was to do the opposite! And that's why you're here, reading *Cool Art*, to learn about the history and key facts of art – in all its wonderful shapes and sizes – so that your imagination is free (but informed) to wander through the landscapes of your favourite artists and ignite your own creative passions.

From Michelangelo to Banksy, Turner to Hirst, Warhol to YOU, making your very own art with your smartphone every single day, art surrounds us everywhere we go and has been a driving force in the intellectual development and evolution of human beings since our ancestors first started drawing stickmen and animals on cave walls over 3,000 years ago. Art has evolved a lot since then.

Cool Art is an exciting history of art, including important artists, ideas and techniques to get you started on a lifelong fascination with art, and artists, of all forms. So, let's get started. Paintbrushes at the ready? Good. Let's go...

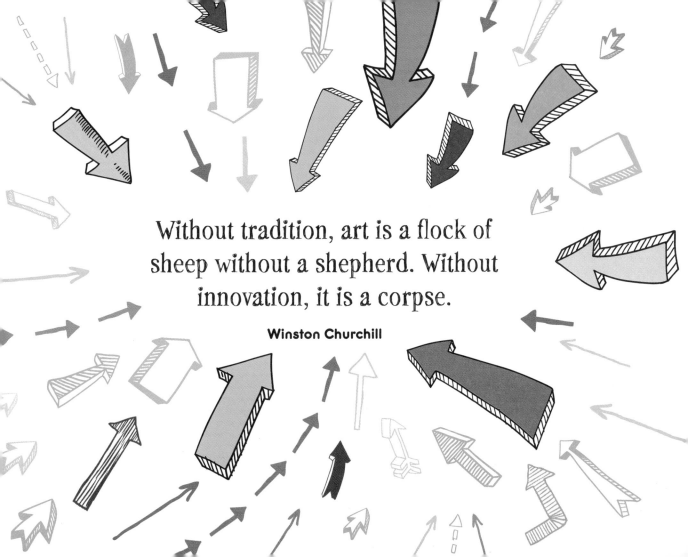

Without tradition, art is a flock of sheep without a shepherd. Without innovation, it is a corpse.

Winston Churchill

The Coolest Art Movements in History

Stone Age (75,000–2,500 BC)
Paleolithic cave people in South Africa create the first known art, by painting images of animals onto rocks. Stonehenge is built in 3000bc too! But is it art?

Baroque (1600–1750)
Art becomes a weapon in religious propaganda. The Dutch Golden Age: Low Country painters Rembrandt, Rubens and Vermeer establish themselves as the greatest painters in the world.

Mesopotamian (3,500–500 BC)
Warrior art!

Early and High Renaissance (1400–1550)
Modern culture is born in Italy, thanks to Leonardo, Donatello, Raphael and Michelangelo, who paints the ceiling of the Sistine Chapel in Vatican City.

Romanticism (1780–1850)
The imagination of the individual becomes key during the French and American Revolutions. Delacroix and Turner are two of the era's heroes.

Roman (500 BC–476 AD)
Romans build the Coliseum and the Pantheon.

Byzantine and Islamic (476–1453 AD)
Mazes, mosaics and the birth of Islam inspire people to pick up a paintbrush.

Realism (1848–1900)
Manet, Courbet and Millet begin work outdoors (*en plein air*) and start a trend for celebrating the working class.

Impressionism (1865–1885)
Capturing the wonder of natural light with Monet, Renoir and Degas.

MODERN ART STARTS!

Surrealism (1917–1950)
Dali twiddles his moustache; Duchamp and Magritte get weird. In 1924 Andre Breton publishes the Surrealist Manifesto.

Pop Art (1954–1970)
Pop culture goes bang! Art as consumerism and fame for 15 minutes for Andy Warhol and Roy Lichtenstein.

Post-Impressionism (1885–1910)
Gently rebelling against Impressionism, van Gogh, Gauguin and Cézanne become legends.

Cubism (1905–1920)
Picasso makes a fine mess with Cubism. Be there or be square!

Abstract Expressionism (1940–1950s)
Expression without form. Put on your overalls – Pollock, de Kooning and Rothko get messy. New York takes the lead over Paris as the global art capital.

Minimalism (1960–1975)
Nothing much to see here.

Expressionism (1900–1935)
Going through the emotions with Expressionists such as Henri Matisse and Wassily Kandinsky.

Postmodernism (1970–)
Damien Hirst drowns a shark!

WHAT'S NEXT?
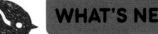

The Great Renaissance
Art is Born Again

COOL MOVEMENTS

Artifacts
Leonardo da Vinci was a painter, sculptor, architect, scientist, mathematician, engineer and anatomist. He has been described as the 'Renaissance Man'.

Renaissance means 'rebirth', and refers to the blossoming resurgence of the arts in Italy from around 1500 AD. The big painters of the Renaissance – Leonardo da Vinci, Michelangelo, Raphael and Titian – have been household names ever since.

Church Influencing Art

During the rise of the Renaissance movement, the Church was extremely powerful and religion dominated daily life in Europe. There was huge demand from the Church for artists to produce work for chapels and cathedrals throughout Italy. So to stay in work, the painters had to produce Christian art, rather than classical subjects from Greece and Rome – that was for pagans.

Keeping it Real

Renaissance painters discovered the rules of perspective, so now paintings looked beautifully realistic. They also got to grips with proportion. Drawing and painting became highly accurate and technical, just like the advances in science and engineering happening at the same time. See page 12 for more on perspective.

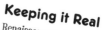

The great and wonderful Renaissance artist Michelangelo – whose works of art quite literally changed the world – started out, in Florence, Italy, as a sculptor. In 1496, he moved to Rome and his *Pietà* – a marble sculpture of the body of Jesus lying in the lap of his mother Mary after the crucifixion – created the following year made his name. A few years later, between 1501 and 1504, he created *David* – his 5m (17ft) tall marble masterpiece of a male nude. But it was with his painting on the ceiling of the Sistine Chapel – including the famous *Creation of Adam* – that saw him instantly become regarded as Italy's greatest artist.

Perspective
Don't Get Stuck in the Background

These days, art doesn't play by the rules. But there is one extremely important set of rules that has survived all the way from the Renaissance to today: perspective.

Before Perspective Happened

Before the 14th century, no one much cared whether objects in the background of paintings appeared smaller than ones in the foreground: most art was depicted on a flat plane, and the size of people and objects were decided according to how important they were.

Perspective is the appearance of things relative to one another as determined by their distance from the viewer. There are two main types of perspective: linear perspective and aerial perspective.

So Why Did it Change?

Then along came Filippo Brunelleschi, an Italian architect. To help him understand the relationship between distance and scale, he painted the outlines of some buildings in Florence onto a mirror, then extended each line back, and found they all converged on the horizon: he had established the idea of the 'vanishing point'. From then onwards, perspective caught on.

Up in the Air
Later in the century, Leonardo da Vinci took matters to a whole new level. At this stage perspective only dealt with rays of light and sightlines, but Da Vinci started thinking about the air through which the light travelled. He noticed that as an object moves further into the distance, its edges blur and it even changes colour. This sort of thing is called 'aerial perspective'.

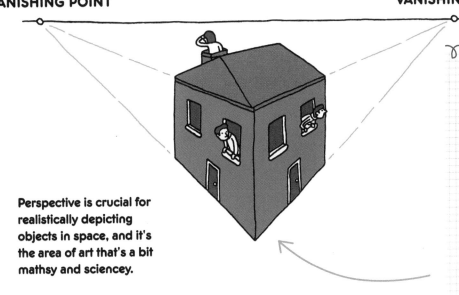

VANISHING POINT

VANISHING POINT

Perspective is crucial for realistically depicting objects in space, and it's the area of art that's a bit mathsy and sciencey.

The Complicated Bit
There are two basic forms of linear perspective:
★ **One-point perspective** happens when the vanishing point is ahead of you; imagine standing on a long straight road looking at the horizon.
★ **Two-point perspective** occurs when looking at an object with two or more sides that are facing you. Like this house right here.

13

Mona Lisa
Leonardo da Vinci

COOL
WORKS OF
ART
#1

Without a doubt, this is one of the most recognisable works of art in the world. Art historians believe the *Mona Lisa* is a portrait of Lisa Gherardini, wife of Francesco del Giocondo, a successful silk merchant from Florence, but she is much more than that...

No Eyebrows, but Such a Lovely Smile

Mona Lisa's 'smile' has been debated and discussed for a hundred years. It's hard to tell whether she is happy or not. The reason for this is actually her eyes, which give no clue as to how she might be feeling. The faint smile on her lips could indicate that she is feeling content, or nervous, or possibly even mischievous – what do *you* think?

Artifacts

The *Mona Lisa* has an imperfection. In 1956, a man named Ugo Ungaza threw a stone at the painting. This resulted in a small patch of damaged paint next to her left elbow.

Louvre at First Sight

In 1911 the *Mona Lisa* was stolen from the Louvre, Paris. The thief, Vincenzo Peruggia, hid in a cupboard overnight, then simply took the painting from the wall and walked out. He was caught two years later when he tried to sell it. He claimed that it wasn't theft at all, but an act of patriotism – he wanted the painting back in Italy. These days, the painting has its own climate-controlled room and is encased in bullet-proof glass.

From whatever angle you look at her, the *Mona Lisa* seems to be looking directly at you. Spooky!

The *Mona Lisa* was painted between 1503 and 1506, and has been hanging at the Louvre since 1797.

No eyebrows! Shaving them off was the done thing in 15th-century Florence.

Leonardo used the blurry *sfumato* effect on the edges of the lips, making them appear lifelike.

No signature! Da Vinci did not sign or date any of his paintings.

Caravaggio
The Bad Boy of Baroque

During an eventful career that only lasted 13 years, when Caravaggio wasn't painting epic masterpieces he could usually be found getting into epic fights and being arrested.

Fights, Paintbrush, Action!

After assaulting a police officer in Milan in 1592, 21-year-old Caravaggio left his hometown for Rome. For his first commission (from the Church, of course) he produced three paintings depicting the life of Saint Matthew, catapulting Caravaggio to stardom as the greatest painter in Rome.

But Caravaggio's eccentric behaviour overshadowed his creative life. He was arrested 11 times in six years, for street brawls and sword fighting, and most famously for throwing an artichoke at a waiter!

In 1606, Caravaggio notoriously killed a man after an argument, and headed into exile in Malta. While he was there, he got into more fights, and even tried to kill one of his minders. Eventually he was pardoned by the Pope, but Caravaggio died of a fever, aged just 38, before he ever made it back home to Rome.

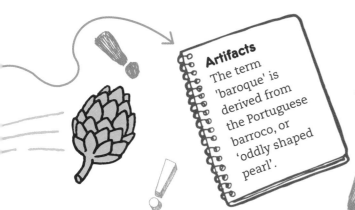

The term 'baroque' is derived from the Portuguese barroco, or 'oddly shaped pearl'.

Light and Dark

Caravaggio's paintings featured graphic scenes of death, nudity and torture, but the most shocking thing was his portrayal of religious figures using ordinary working people as models. This was entirely new, forcing people to reconsider how the world could be represented in painting and changing art forever. He also mastered the technique of *chiaroscuro*, the heavy contrast of light and dark for a dramatic effect.

The Invention of Cropping

Caravaggio was one of the first painters to crop figures in his pictures. While we now think it normal that someone's legs are cut off by a frame, or only part of a person is visible, the idea was seen as the height of weirdness in the 1600s. People would be painted full length and centred. But Caravaggio thought zooming in was the thing.

Rembrandt
The Dutch Master

COOL ARTISTS

The most important artist of the 17th century – during the Dutch Golden Age – and acclaimed for his captivating portraits and mastery of colour, Rembrandt Harmenszoon van Rijn is regarded as one of the greatest European painters in history.

Hailing from a family of millers and bakers, Rembrandt's first foray into art began as a portrait painter. In the mid-1600s, he then got more ambitious, taking on epic scenes, as depicted in one of the world's (and his!) most famous and controversial paintings – the colossal *The Night Watch* (1642). Housed at the Rijksmuseum in Amsterdam, *The Night Watch* displays the captain and company of the civic militia guards who, it is thought, paid Rembrandt 1,600 guilders – this was considered a great deal of money in that era – to paint what would end up one of his finest works.

In spite of his success, Rembrandt lived far beyond his means and was so reckless with money that he spent his last ten years in poverty.

HOW WOULD YOU PAINT YOURSELF?

Artifacts

Rembrandt is most famous for his rather glum-looking self-portraits.

Some of Rembrandt's paintings seem a bit unlucky. *The Night Watch* has been attacked three times: cut with a knife in 1911, very badly slashed in 1975, and sprayed with acid in 1990. Another of his great paintings, *The Storm on the Sea of Galilee* (1633) has been missing since it was stolen from the Isabella Stewart Gardner Museum in Boston, USA, in 1990.

The Big Picture

A Prolific Painter

Rembrandt produced a plethora of paintings and etchings throughout his career. His early painting style was 'smooth', with fine brushwork allowing him to show great detail. In later works his style became rougher, with broader brushstrokes – sometimes he even applied paint using a palette knife. He was also skilled as a printmaker, and again his style evolved as he experimented with different techniques of making marks on plates.

Self-portraits: 40

Paintings: 300

The Rise of the Sculpture
Just Keep Chipping Away

**Sculpture (derived from Latin, meaning 'to carve')
is one of the oldest art forms on earth. Early man used
little statues to bring luck to hunters, then to create
likenesses of gods. And that was just the beginning...**

Life in Three Dimensions

Unlike two-dimensional art on a canvas or screen, which
relies on spatial illusion for its visual impact, a three-
dimensional object challenges and confronts us simply
by being there. It is the powerful, imposing presence
of sculpture that makes a statue the best choice for
'immortalising' famous people in public spaces.

All kinds of natural and industrial materials are used in
sculpture, including stone, metals, ceramics and wood, and
they are shaped using traditional techniques such as stone
carving or bronze casting. Stone is a particularly durable
choice of material, and examples of sculptures made many
thousands of years ago survive today.

**The famous Statue of Liberty, New York, is defined as a
colossal Neoclassical sculpture. How tall do you think it is?**

Sculpture Superlatives

◁▭▭▷ **Oldest** Currently believed to be the *Lion Man*, made from mammoth ivory (yes, *mammoth* ivory) and roughly 40,000 years old. It is 29.6cm (11½ in) high and was found in a cave in Germany.

◁▭▭▷ **Most famous** The *Venus de Milo*, an ancient Greek masterpiece made by (we think) Alexandros of Antioch. And why is this sculpture famous? Because she's armless!

◁▭▭▷ **Most controversial** Stiff competition for this one, but Rodin's *The Kiss* caused a stir everywhere it went in the 19th century because of its steamy and lifelike depiction of, well, a kiss.

◁▭▭▷ **Priciest** Alberto Giacometti's *The Walking Man I* sold for $104.3 million in 2010.

◁▭▭▷ **Tallest** The Spring Temple Buddha stands atop a Buddhist monastery in Lushan County, China. It's enormous, at 153m (502ft), and can be seen from miles around.

Michelangelo's *David*: too rude for this book. See the full monty in the Galleria dell'Accademia, Florence.

Carving out a Place in History

The Western tradition of sculpture began in Ancient Greece and was also popular in the Middle Ages, when religious statues were made in the Gothic style. The Renaissance produced a great number of world-famous sculptures, including Michelangelo's *David*.

Modern sculpture began with Auguste Rodin in 1900, when he exhibited a number of works at the Universal Exhibition in Paris. Rodin's naturalistic style was soon rejected and challenged by Constantin Brancusi's abstract forms, and since then art sculptures have largely abandoned the traditional role of depicting the human body, focusing instead on form, scale and structure.

Answer: 93m (305ft).

JMW Turner
King of the Landscape

Turner was an artist whose skill was apparent from an early age. He revolutionised landscape painting and is still unbeaten in his mastery of watercolour.

A Master at Work

Joseph Mallord William Turner was born in London in 1775 and learned his trade at the Royal Academy. In 1803 he set up his own gallery to show paintings that wouldn't fit in the exhibition room at the Academy, a great way to show off his work and build on his reputation.

Turner began by painting straightforward landscapes and seascapes, but his work gradually evolved as he became increasingly obsessed with the sun and the effects of light. His paintings became huge washes of swirling colour, with bright sunlight and mists obscuring the scene, almost to the point of full abstraction. The loose brushstrokes, highly subjective views and hazy landscapes provoked astonishment and were a huge influence on the Impressionist movement later in the 19th century.

Artifacts
A large portion of Turner's output depicts scenes of catastrophe such as shipwrecks, fires and storms.

'Painting is a strange business.'
J M W Turner

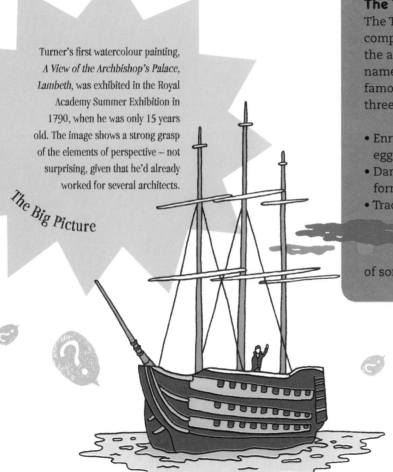

The Big Picture

Turner's first watercolour painting, *A View of the Archbishop's Palace, Lambeth*, was exhibited in the Royal Academy Summer Exhibition in 1790, when he was only 15 years old. The image shows a strong grasp of the elements of perspective – not surprising, given that he'd already worked for several architects.

The Turner Prize

The Turner Prize, the prestigious annual competition for British artists under the age of 50, was created in 1984 and is named in Turner's honour. The prize is famous for its wacky entries. Here are three of the most controversial:

- Enrico David's rocking papier-mâché egg-men
- Damien Hirst's tiger shark encased in formaldehyde
- Tracey Emin's unmade bed

It's interesting to think what Turner himself would have made of some of the winners.

Romanticism
Love is in the air

COOL MOVEMENTS

Romanticism, flowering in the early 19th century, valued human emotions, senses and intuition. It wasn't just an art movement, but involved literature and poetry too.

The Art of Romance

You can apply the term 'Romantic' to any artwork that is guided by feelings and moods rather than the formal structures of classical art. Romanticism is difficult to define, but you could say it's that feeling you get when you're confronted by the immensity of nature, the sort of thing you might experience when arriving at a place of unexpected beauty, looking out onto a raging sea, reaching the top of a mountain and looking down across a valley, or happening upon a picturesque ruin. The renowned Romantic artist Caspar David Friedrich summed up Romanticism by saying 'the artist's feeling is his law'.

Romantic artists were a troubled bunch. To paint his masterpiece *The Raft of the Medusa* (1819), Théodore Géricault shaved off his hair, cut himself off from his friends, stuck a bed in his studio and worked solidly for ten months until he'd finished. Only then did he allow himself the luxury of a nervous breakdown.

The Big Picture

Romanticism's Greatest Hits

▭▭▷ *Tree with Crows* Caspar David Friedrich **1822**

▭▭▷ *Liberty Leading the People* Eugène Delacroix **1830**

▭▭▷ *The Fighting Temeraire Tugged to her Last Berth to be Broken Up* JMW Turner **1839**

▭▭▷ *The Third of May 1808* Francisco Goya **1814**

Romantic-era works of art are renowned for being the first in which landscapes became a significant subject for painting, as opposed to people and scenes.

Realism
Art Imitating Life

Between 1840 and 1880, Realist painters such as Gustave Courbet, Jean-Baptiste-Camille Corot, Jean-François Millet, and Édouard Manet sought to capture reality as accurately as possible, providing the stepping stone for history's next important movement – Modern Art.

Realism – showing things as they are – is the opposite of Idealism, which represents how things *could* or *should* appear.

Great Works of Realism
▻ *The Gleaners* Jean François-Millet 1857
▻ *Young Ladies of the Village* Gustave Courbet 1852
▻ *The Third Class Carriage* Honoré Daumier 1862
▻ *Breakfast in the Studio* Édouard Manet 1868

Artifacts
Realism was an art movement that began in Europe and revolted against the emotional and exaggerated themes of Romanticism. Realists dared to explore the themes of everyday life, and not the fantasy of Idealism or the emotional aspects of Romanticism.

The World as it Really Is
In the 19th century the divide between rich and poor meant that any artist painting things as they really were was bound to be controversial. Gustave Courbet said that all art should show the world as it really was, warts and all, even if that included harrowing depictions of desperately poor people and social injustice.

Manet was another Realist, but he wasn't engaging in social or political issues. *Olympia* (1863), his painting of a naked prostitute on a bed, caused an enormous scandal when it was exhibited at the 1865 Paris Salon.

Édouard Manet: Realist to Impressionist

The Big Picture

Unlike other art movements, there was very little sculpture and architecture produced in the Realist era, perhaps due to the invention of photography in 1840.

'There is only one true thing: instantly paint what you see.'

Édouard Manet

Le Déjeuner sur l'Herbe
Édouard Manet

One of art history's best-known scandals, this painting was rejected by the official Paris Salon jury of 1863 and then shocked viewers while drawing crowds when it was displayed at the *Salon des Refusés*. Why? Partly because it shows a naked woman hanging out with some clothed men, but also because of Manet's revolutionary painting technique.

A New Technique

Manet's painting technique was controversial. By using rapid brushstrokes and blocks of colour, he made no attempt to merge tones to create a conventional illusion. The art establishment of the time thought this was just laziness, but it was an entirely deliberate technique devised by the artist. And what's more, it proved a heavy influence on the Impressionist movement, which was to follow shortly...

The naked woman looks out of the painting to meet the eye of the viewer. This was a problem for some, especially the Salon's jury, who weren't used to seeing women looking so brazen. Manet was challenging the viewer, asking us to consider the relationship between observing and being observed.

Artifacts

In English the painting's title translates as 'The Luncheon on the Grass', though was originally titled *Le Bain*, or 'The Bath'.

28

Famous Impressionist artist Claude Monet's own version of *Le Déjeuner sur l'Herbe* (1865–1866), was inspired by Manet's original masterpiece.

The painting is packed with art-history references to the Italian Renaissance. The men in the painting are a reworking of Raphael's river gods, recast as respectable middle-to-upper-class gentlemen.

Lens! Camera! Action!
Taking Pictures

Photography, the process of capturing light onto film, was one of Man's greatest technological advances. It became the new way to document the world and made a large part of painting redundant almost instantly.

Artifacts
The word 'photography', from the Greek words *photos* ('light') and *graphein* ('to draw') was first used by scientist Sir John FW Herschel in 1839.

The Death of Painting?

In the mid-1800s, many people assumed the lens might replace the paintbrush entirely, but painting survived, although art itself was fundamentally changed by the invention of the camera. It is no coincidence that the highly subjective, anti-realist movement of Impressionism started at the same time as photography went mainstream. Photography may have inadvertently given birth to Modern Art.

> 'Your first 10,000 photographs are your worst.'
> **Henri Cartier-Bresson**

> 'There are no bad pictures: that's just how your face looks sometimes.'
> **Abraham Lincoln**

CLICK!

Painting Versus Art

Photography changed artists' sense of composition. A camera's viewfinder reminds us that the image continues outside the frame and we can choose which part of the scene to photograph. After photography came along, painting started to move away from capturing the centre of the frame, hence the move to more extreme techniques and styles, as displayed in Modern Art.

The Camera Never Lies?

In terms of documentary truth, photographs appear more reliable than paintings, but everyone knows cameras can lie too. Photographers can choose what to point the camera at, when to take a shot, and, crucially, can decide which elements to leave in or miss out. On top of that, they can select a single picture that may appear to tell a very different story to others taken at the same time.

The first ever colour photograph was taken in 1861 by Thomas Sutton, using a three-colour process devised by British physicist James Clark Maxwell. The photograph was of a tartan ribbon.

The Big Picture

Still Life With Seven Apples
Paul Cézanne

Paul Cézanne once declared: 'With an apple I will astonish Paris.' And he did. A master of illusion, he's often considered the most influential painter of the late 19th century. Pablo Picasso referred to him as 'the father of us all'.

A is for Apple

While his associates and friends in the Impressionist movement in Paris were principally concerned with light and colour, Cézanne was much more interested in form. He chose to paint the apples because he wished to elevate humble subjects, such as apples, to the same status as the religious subjects of the Old Masters he had spent years studying.

Artifacts

Historians believe Cézanne is the bridge between Impressionism and Cubism, the movement of the early 20th century.

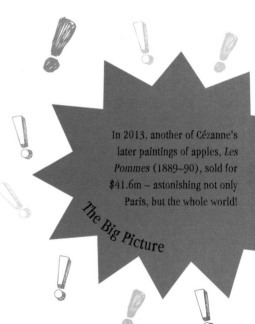

In 2013, another of Cézanne's later paintings of apples, *Les Pommes* (1889–90), sold for $41.6m – astonishing not only Paris, but the whole world!

The Big Picture

Stand back... and watch the apples magically turn three-dimensional!

How to Paint Still Life like Paul Cézanne

1 Pick an object, like a ball or a glass or a chair.

2 Place your object on a table or counter. Make sure the background isn't complicated.

3 Locate a light source, such as a lamp, and shine it on your object in the way you want.

4 After choosing your location, look at your object from all angles for a few minutes. Try to establish in your mind the position, shading, texture and look you are going for.

5 As you begin, try using shapes that you see in the object, such as circles or rectangles, or draw light lines that divide the object equally.

6 Once you have the drawn the entire object lightly, start darkening the outlines, but not so dark that it makes it look two-dimensional.

7 Now start adding details, like shading.

8 When that's done, take a step back and look at your picture, compared to the object. What else needs doing? Get on with it then!

Primary Colours

The way colours work is crucial to art: some artists are fascinated by the effects of light; some are interested in the symbolic meaning of colour; and some use colour to express their emotions. But it all starts with the primary colours.

Palettes at the Ready...

Primary colours
Red, yellow and blue.

Secondary colours
Made from an equal mixture of two primary colours: violet (blue and red), green (blue and yellow), orange (red and yellow).

Tertiary colours
A mixture of a primary colour and one of its secondaries, such as a blue-violet or a blue-green.

> 'A thimbleful of red is redder than a bucketful.'
> **Henri Matisse**

Yellow

Yellow represents happiness, energy and light, but also sickness. Van Gogh and Monet adored yellow and used it often, but Degas thought it horrible and couldn't bear to use it.

Red

Red is not only a primary, it is a primal colour. Red is the colour of anger, blood, heat, love and passion, so it's no surprise that it is a popular choice for artists. It was one of the first colours to be used in painting, with tones extracted from clay, lead and mercury ore. A very bright red, Carmine, was made from mashed-up female cochineal beetles. Carmine is still used today as a food colouring (E120).

> 'If you see a tree as blue, then make it blue.'
> **Paul Gauguin**

Blue

The French painter Yves Klein saw blue as a colour of great spiritual meaning. He used it as a symbol of the immaterial, the void. The colour meant so much to him that he attempted to have his favourite ultramarine shade copyrighted and trademarked. While exposure to the colour blue is said to lift the spirits, it is also well known for its melancholy effects. Pablo Picasso's so-called 'Blue Period', between 1901 and 1904, refers to a series of paintings he completed that were dominated by the colour blue and inspired by his depression.

Complementary Colours

**There is so much you can do with colour.
There's a whole spectrum at your disposal.**

Opposites Attract

Every colour has an opposite, called a complement.
The colour wheel is a simple way to show colour
complements. Artists use complements to great
effect. For example, if red appears in a picture,
the eye will automatically start looking for green
among any other colours present: the green makes
the red appear more intense.
And if an artist wants to make
a woman's orange hair
dazzlingly bright, making
her outfit and earrings blue
will do the trick.

**The Colour Wheel –
invented by Sir Isaac Newton!**

'Colour is the place
where our brain and
the universe meet.'
Paul Klee

Colourful Terms to Learn

'The purest and most thoughtful minds are those which love colour the most.'
John Ruskin

Hue
The strength of a single colour from full saturation down to white. The word is used to suggest that the colour we see is not at its full strength.

Tone
The degree of darkness from black to white. In a black-and-white photograph you are able to see and understand the image independently of colour. The word 'shade' is often used in place of 'tone'.

Does Colour Exist?
No, it doesn't. Colour is manufactured in our brains. Our impression of colour results from the division of light into separate wavelengths, which creates the visible spectrum. Our brains translate these wavelengths into colours.

Black and White

'If I could find anything blacker than black,
I would use it.'

JMW Turner

'White can be attained by blending all the colours of the spectrum together, or through the subtraction of ink and all other pigments. White is 'all colours' and 'no colour' at the same time.'

Kenya Hara

Impressionism
Blurred Vision

COOL MOVEMENTS

Impressionism took the focus of art away from the subject and back to the artist. The Impressionists' aim was to capture a moment in time, and the light and colour of that moment was more important to them than the details of what they were painting.

Artifacts
The painting characteristics of Impressionism included small, thin, yet visible brushstrokes, open composition, emphasis on accurate depiction of light, common subject matter, a degree of movement of the subjects and unusual visual angles.

The Artist's Back in Charge!
The Realism movement had changed the subject of art, but not the method. Impressionism came next, and it disregarded any attempts at painting objective truths. The Impressionists believed the world should be painted subjectively, as perceived by the individual artist, and becoming far removed from any traditional rules. From Impressionism onwards, artists had complete stylistic freedom. While critics at the time were not impressed with Impressionism, the artists never looked back.

The term 'Impressionism' was derived from Monet's painting *Impression, Sunrise* (1872), which depicted a seascape of the port at Le Havre. When the painting was exhibited in 1874, art critic Louis Leroy read the painting's title and a new art movement was born.

The Big Picture

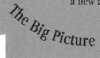

Great Impressionist Works

✏️ *The Absinthe Drinker* Edgar Degas **1876**

✏️ *Luncheon of the Boating Party* Pierre-Auguste Renoir **1881**

✏️ *Paris Street; Rainy Day* Gustave Caillebotte **1877**

✏️ *Impression, Sunrise* Claude Monet **1872**

✏️ *Water Lilies* Claude Monet after **1916**

'Impressionism is the newspaper of the soul.'
Henri Matisse

IMPRESSIONISTS ALWAYS PACKED AN UMBRELLA

Impressionists painted in all weathers.

It's all about the light.

Claude Monet
The Impressionist Dandy

The characteristic style of Monet and his friends, who liked nothing more than lounging around outside with their easels, has produced one of the most admired and influential art movements in history.

Artifacts

Monet's most famous series of paintings, Water Lilies, took 10 years to complete. There were 250 individual paintings.

'The richness I achieve comes from nature, the source of my inspiration.'
Claude Monet

'Impressionism? I invented that!'

How to Paint Like Monet

It's easy if you know how. OK, it's not that easy, but here are the basics to get you started:

1 Use a coloured canvas background. This helps take the glare off a boring white canvas and gives you a tone to start off with.

2 Using a 3B pencil, draw the basic shapes of the piece you wish to create, be it a mountain, a sky or a bunch of flowers.

3 Prepare your palette. Replicate the colours you see onto your palette, using complementary colours and the colour wheel.

4 Paint in the basic colours first, such as a cobalt blue sky or a grassy green field.

5 Create colour harmony. Use your palette to start mixing colours to match what you see. Start adding dabs of heavy colour on prominent areas of block colours, and tone colours down with other lighter colours, boldly dashing the paint on the canvas as you see fit.

6 Be quick! Make sure you get up nice and early to take advantage of the sunlight.

> 'Colours pursue me like a constant worry. They even worry me in my sleep.'
> **Claude Monet**

A Breath of Fresh Air

The term *en plein air* means 'in the open air' and refers to the Impressionists' habit of painting outdoors. Monet would often set up four separate canvases beside each other and paint each of them at different times of day. He'd end up with four paintings of the same scene painted at different times.

The Big Art Debate

This discussion has been ongoing for decades. Should art be engaged with, or detached from, politics and society? What do you think?

2B or not 2B: The Argument

There are two sides in this debate:

1. If artists don't address important political and moral matters, then their work can only be perceived as an indulgent waste of time, with no larger importance to the wider world.

2. Art should *only* be concerned with timeless beauty, and bringing pleasure and escapism from the everyday political, moral and social problems of 'real life'.

The Two Sides of the Argument

German philosopher Immanuel Kant said that beauty, and therefore art, must be detached from matters of morality. The creation of art is for no other purpose than itself: 'art for art's sake'.

Russian novelist Leo Tolstoy objected furiously to this. In his essay 'What Is Art?', written in 1896, he argued that the sole function of art was to convey moral values, and not beauty; art was only valuable when it communicated a moral idea, and art for mere pleasure or amusement was not real art. For Tolstoy, if art didn't instruct and moralise, it was just decoration.

French poet and writer Théophile Gautier argued 'there is nothing truly beautiful that can be used for anything. Everything that is useful is ugly, for it is the expression of some need'. For Gautier, real art has no use – it is only about beauty.

Drawing the Line

Expecting artists to deal only with beauty and keep out of politics is a useful way for powerful elites to keep creative people, who historically have seen it as their role to rally against authorities and the establishment, quiet. However, dismissing artists for only dealing with beauty when there are terrible events occurring in the world is also problematic. It's a totally polarised argument, and as always in these cases, both positions are valid.

We don't have to choose: art can still progress despite conflicting schools of thought. Where do you stand?

Picasso is a good example of an artist who has produced art that presents a political and moral opinion, and also work that was concerned purely with technique and form.

The Big Picture

'All art is quite useless.'
Oscar Wilde

'Art, like morality, consists of drawing the line somewhere.'
GK Chesterton

The Starry Night
Vincent van Gogh

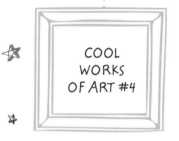

COOL WORKS OF ART #4

Van Gogh painted *The Starry Night* while staying at a psychiatric hospital in Saint-Rémy-de-Provence in the south of France in 1889, suffering from severe depression. A year after completing this masterpiece, van Gogh was found dead by an apparent gunshot wound – mystery still surrounds how he died.

Ear We Go...

Everyone knows about van Gogh's left ear. The usual story is that, after an argument with fellow artist Paul Gauguin, he cut it off in a drunken rage. But there's a different version: it seems the dispute was over the affections of a prostitute called Rachel. At the time, the two artists had been painting in a bullring in Arles. Tradition said that a victorious bullfighter got the ear of the bull as a trophy. When Gauguin charmed Rachel, van Gogh gave her his ear to show she had been a successful matador.

Artifacts

The Starry Night has striking similarities to a sketch of the Whirlpool Galaxy, 24 million light years from Earth and drawn by Lord Rosse 44 years before Van Gogh's work.

Though the picture is of the nighttime, Van Gogh painted it, from memory, during the day. This technique adds to the dreamlike mood of the painting.

The sky, more like a firework display than a quiet night in rural France, hints at van Gogh's mental state while painting the picture. Is the picture a projection of the artist's troubled mind, filled with hallucinatory visions and nostalgic imaginings, or is it simply a spirited attempt to paint in a way that grabs attention?

The view is from the window of his room, where we can see the cypress trees and jagged Provençal hillsides beneath an extraordinary and fantastic swirl of stars. But the village in the valley below is not Saint-Rémy. It's not even French. The church spire and the buildings around it are Dutch: a homage to van Gogh's origins in Holland. Mixing the two places together may have a sentimental purpose for van Gogh and adds to the overall bewitching aura of the painting.

COOL ARTISTS

Kazimir Malevich
An Art Revolutionary

19th-century Russian painter Kazimir Malevich set out to separate art from real-life objects. Rather radically, he attempted to eradicate all reference to reality and representation in his painting.

Malevich studied art in Moscow and was influenced by Cubism and the avant-garde artists of the time. Shaken by the events of the First World War and the political situation in Russia, he felt that no artistic movement was portraying the things that interested him. In 1915 he published his manifesto, *From Cubism to Suprematism*, which established Suprematism as an art movement. In the same year, he exhibited his painting *Black Square on a White Ground*, which made him the figurehead of the Russian avant-garde and a pioneer of abstract art and minimalism.

Malevich carried on with his career under communism, in spite of the regime's suspicion of artists that were not fully supportive of their Social Realist style. Later on, under Stalin, the government became more intolerant of the abstract style and Malevich was banned from creating and exhibiting abstract works. He died in Leningrad (St Petersburg) in 1935.

Upon unveiling his infamous *Black Square* in 1916, Malevich declared the square to be the 'face of the new art … the first step of pure creation.'

But is it Art?

Observed across a room, *Black Square* is a solid and impenetrable black mass. It represents the end of content, the end of colour, and is just a flat surface. There is nothing to see, and it forces the viewer to consider nothingness and eternity. The black square is like a full stop at the end of representational art. However, when you examine the painting up close, you can see that it is not a solid black mass at all, but that it contains brushstrokes, blotches, and, crucially, variation. This is the brilliance of the painting: if it had been produced mathematically and technically, it would have failed as a work of art. But because it is imperfect, and human, this painting is full of optimism.

'Colour is the essence of painting, which the subject always killed.'
Kazimir Malevich

The Big Picture

Malevich was the oldest of 14 children. He was brought upin the Ukraine and knew nothing about artists until the age of 12, although he did enjoy a bit of embroidery.

Cubism
The Building Blocks of Modern Art

COOL MOVEMENTS

The pioneers of Cubism looked for new ways to depict three-dimensional subjects on a flat canvas, and this helped them pave the way for many other 20th-century modern art movements.

Dismantling the View

While Edvard Munch and the Expressionists were busy putting their emotions and feelings onto canvas, back in Paris, Pablo Picasso and Georges Braque were more concerned with 'dismantling' various objects, notably faces and musical instruments, and then rearranging them on the canvas. The effect was of an object being viewed from several angles at the same time – alien, but effective. Cubism, the first abstract/avant-garde movement of the 20th century, broke away from the principles of perspective that had been adhered to for 400 years, and another major art movement was born. Cubism, though responsible for many of the world's bestselling prints, didn't last long but it did help pave the way for Surrealism. And then things *really* started to get cool...

'Cubism is the art of painting original arrangements composed of elements taken from conceived rather than perceived reality.'
Guillaume Apollinaire

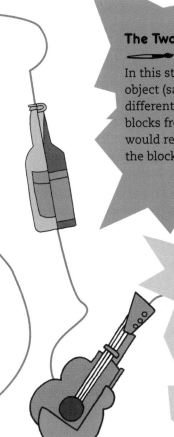

The Two Stages of Cubism

➤ 1. Analytical Cubism
In this style, artists would study the object (say, a violin) and break it up into different blocks. They would look at the blocks from different angles. Then they would reconstruct the subject, painting the blocks from various viewpoints.

➤ 2. Synthetic Cubism
This simpler, lighter and brighter stage introduced the idea of artists using coloured paper, newspapers and other materials to represent the different blocks of the subject.

Cubism's Greatest Hits
▭➤ *Les Demoiselles d'Avignon* Pablo Picasso **1907**
▭➤ *La Femme au Cheval* Jean Metzinger **1911–1912**
▭➤ *Nude Descending a Staircase, No. 2* Pablo Picasso **1912**
▭➤ *Man with a Guitar* Georges Braque **1914**
▭➤ *Three Musicians* Pablo Picasso **1921**

Pablo Picasso
A 20th-century Legend

COOL ARTISTS

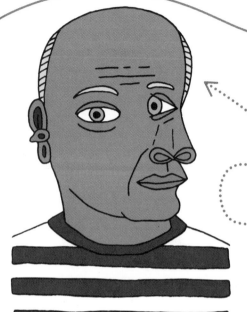

Picasso's inventiveness, creative energy, his talent in painting, drawing and sculpture, his rejection of middle-class values, his politics and his profilic productivity, make him one of the greatest artists ever.

Picasso Checklist – How Much do you Know?

❑ As a child, Picasso's first word was 'pencil'.

❑ His father trained him in drawing when he was seven years old, and he completed his first painting when he was nine.

❑ Aged 15, he passed the month-long entrance exam for Madrid's Royal Academy on the first day.

❑ Picasso moved to Paris in 1901, where he soon began to make a name for himself (although he was so poor during this time he was burning his old paintings just to keep warm!)

❑ While working with Braque around 1909, Picasso invented Cubism, the controversial style that would define him.

'Painting was not invented to decorate homes. It is a weapon of attack and defence against the enemy.'
Pablo Picasso

'When I was a child my mother said to me, "If you become a soldier, you'll be a general. If you become a monk, you'll be the pope." Instead I became a painter and wound up as Picasso.'

Pick up a Picasso – the Artist's Most Famous Works

- Les Demoiselles d'Avignon 1907
- Nude, Green Leaves and Bust 1932
- Asleep 1932
- Le Rêve (The Dream) 1932
- Blue Nude 1902
- Dora Maar au Chat 1941
- Seated Woman (Marie-Therese) 1937
- The Old Guitarist 1903
- Girl Before A Mirror 1932
- Three Musicians 1921

A lifelong communist, Picasso refused to fight in either of the world wars or the Spanish Civil War. His masterpiece, a huge mural called Guernica, was Picasso's politically charged response to General Franco's bombings of the Basque town in 1937. Some years later, a Gestapo officer was harassing Picasso in Nazi-occupied Paris. He pointed to a photograph of Guernica and asked, 'Did you do this?' Picasso replied, 'No, you did!'

The Big Picture

Sending Messages
Revealing, Decoding, Communicating

What is the main point of art? For most of us, art is about sending and expressing a visual message that communicates our emotions directly and succinctly.

These messages can be transmitted in three ways:

1. Presentational
As a primary source, by the voice, or by facial expressions or body language.

2. Representational
As a secondary source, through paintings, drawings, books and photographs.

3. Mechanical
Through telephones, the Internet, television, radio and cinema.

Art is usually representational: there is a primary message being transmitted via an artist onto a secondary medium.

The Big Picture

Adults tend to become more risk-averse as they get older, so they develop familiar routines and stick to them. It is the same with art and representation: adults often need to have the meaning of a piece of art explained to them. In contrast, children are literal in their approach to perception, but naïve about convention. Consequently, they often devise highly creative forms of representation and make much better artists and art critics than adults.

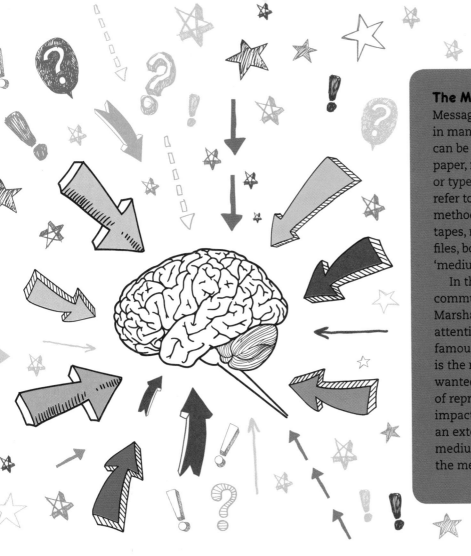

The Medium is the Message

Messages can be represented in many different ways. A story can be written on a sheet of paper, read out on the radio, or typed into a computer. We refer to each of these delivery methods – artworks, cassette tapes, magazines, films, MP3 files, books and signposts – as 'mediums'.

In the mid-1960s, the communication theorist Marshall McLuhan drew attention to mediums with his famous quote 'The medium is the message'. McLuhan wanted to show that the choice of representation affected the impact of the message to such an extent that the chosen medium was as important as the message itself.

Surrealism
Unlocking
the Unconscious

Artifacts
The Surrealist movement began in the 1920s, led by the poet and writer André Breton, as a way to find truth in the world through the subconscious mind and dreams, as opposed to logical thought.

Surrealism tends to be thought of as an 'anything goes', anarchic style, but a good way to think of Surrealism is via its translation from the French: 'beyond realism'.

Welcome to the Weird!

Surrealism ushered in an age of embracing your inner weirdo, but the movement was actually borne out of two significant – and rather serious – events that influenced popular culture at large:

1. The popularity of Sigmund Freud's psychoanalytic studies of irrationality and the unconscious mind.
2. The aftermath of the First World War, which led Surrealists to reject the importance of dominant ideas of enlightened civilisation and human reason and indulge in the strange surroundings of the human subconciousness.

Wonky elephants

trombones for heads ...

human fish ...

Surrealists' artworks differ enormously from anything that had come before: they can include a mix of collage, painting, photography and film. They are also usually themed around dreams, fantasies, sexuality, randomness and taboo subjects.

The Big Picture

Free your Mind

André Breton insisted that Surrealism was not just a new type of creative expression, but a path to total liberation of the mind. The way to become free was to unlock the unconscious mind through free association of ideas. So Surrealists tried outlandish techniques such as automatic writing, in which you subconsciously write words on paper without thinking about it, to help them make purer art.

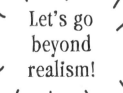

Let's go beyond realism!

Salvador Dalí
Hand-painted
Dream Photographs

Artifacts
Salvador Dalí produced more than 1500 paintings in his lifetime, many of which included the repeated imagery of melting clocks, elephants, eggs, ants, snails and locusts!

An artist with a rich imagination, and a famous moustache, Dalí is best known for his strange and hyperreal paintings, but he also designed the Chupa Chups lollipops logo!

Who the Devil was Dalí?

Dalí was born exactly nine months after the death of his older brother, and his parents gave him the same name as the son they lost. This had quite an effect on Dalí, who grew up imagining he was the reincarnated spirit of his brother. So he became obsessed with the ideas of death and decay, which certainly showed up on his canvases later.

Away from this darker side, Dalí was extremely confident as a young boy. By the age of ten, he declared himself to be a genius, and took up painting. He began with an Impressionist style, then dallied with Cubism and Dadaism before finding Surrealism. Never backward in coming forward, he was expelled from art school in Madrid for telling his teachers he was smarter than all of them would ever be.

In 1927 he moved to Paris and took up with André Breton's Surrealist movement. This was when he created his best work – the strange, dreamlike paintings everyone knows. By 1934, a dubious fascination with Franco and Hitler led to him being expelled from the Surrealist group. In 1940 he left Paris for the United States, where he was treated like a celebrity: he was known as 'Mr Surrealism' and lived the sort of life he had always imagined, that of an acclaimed and successful artistic genius. When he returned to Spain in 1948 he was a household name.

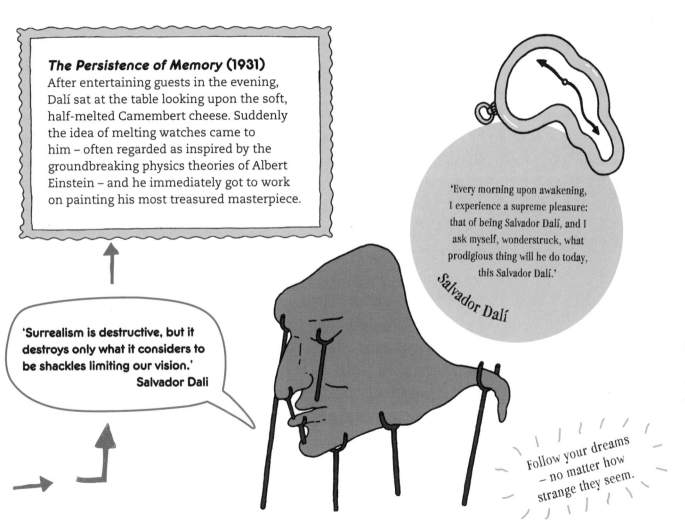

The Persistence of Memory (1931)
After entertaining guests in the evening, Dalí sat at the table looking upon the soft, half-melted Camembert cheese. Suddenly the idea of melting watches came to him – often regarded as inspired by the groundbreaking physics theories of Albert Einstein – and he immediately got to work on painting his most treasured masterpiece.

'Every morning upon awakening, I experience a supreme pleasure: that of being Salvador Dalí, and I ask myself, wonderstruck, what prodigious thing will he do today, this Salvador Dalí.'
Salvador Dalí

'Surrealism is destructive, but it destroys only what it considers to be shackles limiting our vision.'
Salvador Dali

Follow your dreams – no matter how strange they seem.

COOL WORKS OF ART #5

Fountain
Marcel Duchamp

OK, it's a urinal. But is it? Marcel Duchamp's *Fountain* was a defining moment in modern art, and its impact still influences all areas of art theory and practice today. How is it possible that a generic porcelain urinal could single-handedly cause a revolution in art?

Art or Plumbing?

In 1917, Duchamp found the urinal in a hardware store in New York. He bought it, took it to his studio, turned it upside down, put it on a plinth, signed it and declared it art. It was a bit of an infantile gesture, intended to provoke people, but he may have been right. Could his urinal be art?

Duchamp's practical joke-turned-concept caused havoc in the art world. He submitted *Fountain* for the annual exhibition of the American Society of Independent Artists, but it was refused on the grounds of indecency and also plagiarism, because the object had been made by a plumber rather than an artist.

Artifacts
The original version of *Fountain*, according to Duchamp's biographer, was thrown away after someone mistook it for rubbish!

The original *Fountain* disappeared, but this wasn't a problem for Duchamp, because he could just go back to the hardware store and buy another one. There are now 15 urinals in the world regarded as Duchamp fountains, all handmade copies of the non-handmade original!

The Big Picture

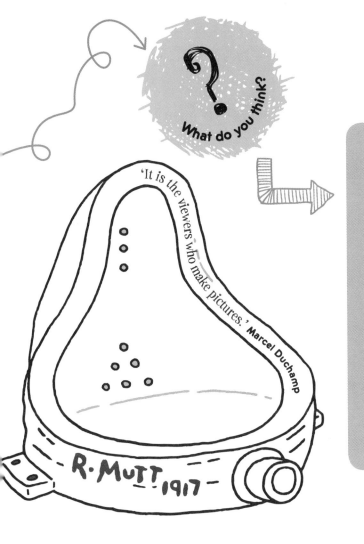

What do you think?

'It is the viewers who make pictures.' Marcel Duchamp

R.MUTT 1917

Original Urinal

By taking a functional object and making it useless by calling it art, Duchamp raised a number of rather profound questions.

➤ What right does an artist have to declare something to be art?
➤ What right do institutions have to judge?
➤ What are the basic characteristics of an artwork?
➤ Does art have to be produced by an artist, or can a pre-made object be art?

Whether Fountain is a work of art or not, its presence provokes good questions without providing answers, an approach since emulated by many artists.

Can Art Change Your Life?

Have you ever felt confused in a gallery? Have you wondered why the person next to you is staring so intently at a splash of paint on a canvas? Why aren't you enjoying yourself as much as they are? Here's how we can appreciate art as fully as possible.

1 Be Confident in Your Opinion

Your opinion counts, no matter how silly or uneducated you think it might be. It's natural to be suspicious of people who claim that a painting, a poem or a song has 'changed their lives', especially when they are people you have known both before and after this so-called profound experience, and you can't see any difference.

To appear cultured and intelligent, we are supposed to know a bit about art, and be able to articulate an opinion on it. How can we do that, if all we see is a pile of bricks on the floor or a black square on a white background?

Nobody wants to look, or feel, stupid, but many people become unsure and uncomfortable in an art gallery. Some people pretend to know lots about a subject when they don't, and some people who don't know anything about a subject reject it as unimportant. Neither of these responses help us get any closer to our profound experience. If you don't understand something, it's best to say so, or say nothing! Then use this experience to become informed so you can remember what you learnt next time around.

> Find the meaning that's true to you.

> 'If you hear a voice within you say "you cannot paint," then by all means paint, and that voice will be silenced.'
> **Vincent van Gogh**

> 'Imagination is more important than knowledge.'
> **Albert Einstein**

Your art motto:
Engage and find out
Dismiss and lose out

2 How Open is your Mind?

Not all art is great. And it's not just you that's confused either. Even famous art critics don't 'get' works of art that are perceived as masterpieces. The painting on the wall in front of you may well be total rubbish. So let's set aside self-conscious fears and start looking and finding out more.

Many artworks deliberately set out to test us to see exactly how open our minds can be, so be patient and see what happens. The philosopher Arthur Schopenhauer once said 'we should comfort ourselves with the masterpieces of art as with exalted personages – stand quietly before them and wait until they speak to us'.

3 Education and Interpretation

Engage with the artwork, find out about the artist, the ideas, the historical context, the symbolic references. If this information isn't available, have a go at interpretation. Simply allow yourself to think about what you are looking at. Maybe squint, frown or stare intently at a part of the work no one else would think is important. If we assume everything is there for a reason, that includes all the small details. Is there a story here? What is the subject? Are there any symbols? How was this piece made? Does the place where the work is situated affect the work itself? Why has the artist chosen to use those particular colours or tones?

By the time you've done all of that, you might find you actually do like it after all. You may even find yourself in the warm and fuzzy embrace of a profound experience of art!

The Treachery of Images
René Magritte

One of Belgian Surrealist René Magritte's key works is a painting of a pipe. Written underneath are the words 'Ceci n'est pas une pipe' ('This is not a pipe'). But if isn't a pipe, what is it?

Virtual Reality

The correct answer would be that it is a representation, a painting of a pipe: a painting of a pipe is not an actual pipe. The same can be said for the word 'pipe'. 'Pipe' isn't an actual pipe either, but simply a word that stands for the presence (or absence) of a real pipe. The painting calls everyday reality into question, implying that evidence we often so readily accept may be fake or illusory. It is about language and images, truth and falsity.

Because painting, language and photographs are secondary ways of representing primary reality, they can be unreliable. Magritte is reminding us not to confuse representation with reality. It is reckless to discuss representation in terms of truth and falsity. However, it is still true to say that the image in Magritte's painting looks like a pipe, and it would be a lie to say it didn't. While representation can be unreliable, it performs an essential function: we all need a language of signs, symbols and words.

Artifacts

Painted in 1928, Magritte's pipe was an instant classic. But he was also famous for *The Son of Man*, *Golconda* and *The Mysteries of the Horizon*. Check them out!

...and this isn't smoke, either.

'Art evokes the mystery without which the world would not exist.'
René Magritte

Magritte's painting was first exhibited in 1933 at the Palais des Beaux-Arts in Brussels, and was praised by Salvador Dalí. Three years later, at the same venue, Magritte went further with his theme of word and image confusion by placing a picture of a piece of cheese in a gold frame under a glass cheese dome, and calling it 'This is a Piece of Cheese.'

The Big Picture

Art as representation

The World's Greatest Galleries

There are many amazing galleries and museums around the world, and between them these galleries contain examples of some of the greatest artwork ever created.

Tate Modern, London

Over 5 million visitors per year
Taking over an enormous disused power station by the River Thames in the year 2000, Tate Modern promptly became the most-visited gallery dedicated to modern art. Its collection of international art is proudly displayed across seven floors, with exhibitions always happening alongside the vast permanent   collection. It
is also one of   London's most
popular places to   hang out in.

Louvre, Paris, France

Over 9 million visitors per year
The most visited art museum in the world, the Louvre was originally built in 1190 as a huge fortress to prevent the Normans invading Paris. In 1358, Charles V turned it into a royal palace. After Louis XIV moved to Versailles, the building was unused until the French Revolution, when it was opened to the public as a gallery for the royal art collection. Critical to the Louvre's success is their possession of the *Mona Lisa*. And it's got a really cool glass pyramid in the middle.

Metropolitan Museum of Art, New York, USA

Over 6 million visitors per year
Known as the 'Met', this museum was set up in 1870 by a group of artists and businesses. At first it held a small collection of European paintings, but now has a collection that spans centuries, from early Islamic and Egyptian pieces through to contemporary works. The savvy business brain of the museum endures: they have a policy of selling off lesser-known works to raise funds to buy masterpieces.

Uffizi, Florence, Italy

1.7 million visitors per year
Built by the Medici family to house their vast collection of art, including pieces by Caravaggio, Dürer, Michelangelo, Raphael and Titian, the Uffizi opened in 1591, making it the oldest public museum in the world. It is huge, and the sheer quantity and scale of the art on display can be overwhelming. Titian's *Venus of Urbino*, Caravaggio's *Medusa* and Botticelli's *The Birth of Venus* can all be seen here. Anna Maria Ludovica, the last heir of the Medici family, gave generously to the charity and made a legal pact with Italy to ensure all the Uffizi's art would belong to the city of Florence forever.

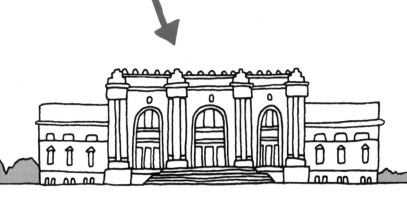

Frida Kahlo
Art and Pain

Frida Kahlo remains one of South America's most treasured Surrealist painters. Born in Mexico City, Kahlo experienced suffering and tragedy throughout her life, but eventually became internationally renowned for her self-portraits – though sadly not until decades after her own death.

COOL ARTISTS

'I paint myself because I am so often alone and because I am the subject I know best.'
Frida Kahlo

Artifacts

In 1925, Frida Kahlo (1907–54) was a promising medical student at the National University in Mexico. One day, the bus she was riding home from college collided with a tram. Several people were killed, and the impact left Kahlo close to death with a broken spine, collarbone, ribs, pelvis and legs. Several months of hospital recovery and operations followed, and during this time Kahlo took up painting to distract her from her pain and to relieve the boredom of being bedridden.

That Frida Feeling

Frida lied about her birthday so she could claim her birthday began in the same year as the Mexican Revolution, so we'd better get our facts straight. Let's consult our Kahlo Checklist:

❏ Born in 1907, not 1910 as she claimed.

❏ Frida Kahlo was a surrealist painter, known for her self-portraits.

❏ André Breton, the artist who pioneered the Surrealist movement, described Kahlo's work as like 'a ribbon around a bomb'.

❏ Mexican culture and tradition is an important stylistic and thematic feature in Kahlo's work.

❏ Many of Kahlo's paintings deal with her relationship with her famous Mexican painter husband, Diego Rivera, and her experiences of the streetcar accident that changed her life.

❏ Kahlo's self-portraits suggest a fusion of styles such as Christian and Aztec imagery and knowledge of European art.

❏ One of Kahlo's most revered self-portraits was *The Broken Column*, which depicted the artist's own inner pain, an image of her broken body held together by a harness.

Kahlo painted many self-portraits and pictures that illustrated her life, family and experiences, all influenced by Mexican folk art and mural painting. She later married Mexico's most celebrated artist and muralist, Diego Rivera. Their relationship was a tempestuous one.

The Big Picture

Cool Kahlo Works

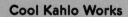 *Self Portrait in a Velvet Dress* 1926

Self Portrait with Thorn Necklace and Hummingbird 1940

The Suicide of Dorothy Hale 1938

Self Portrait with the Portrait of Doctor Farill 1951

The Usual Suspects

As well as being full of art, galleries are also filled with a lot of hot air generated by the people who visit. Let us now deconstruct the four common phrases – and responses – you'll hear at every art gallery. By doing this we can shine a light on the common ways in which art is appreciated, or dismissed – perhaps without a true understanding of the artist's intention.

'You must create'.
Raymond Loewy

'I could do that!'
It's easy to say you (or your five-year-old) could have done better, but until you actually make something, then you'll always be a spectator and never an artist. In art, action is the point – doing and making. Great artists make difficult things appear easy – could you *really* have done that?

'I don't know much about art, but I know what I like.'
Art almost always tries to make the viewer think in a new way. If you use this well-trodden cliché, it sounds like you're not open to new ideas and, worse, not even trying to understand the artwork. Sure, say you don't like it after you've looked at it (that is allowed), but don't dismiss it before you've even tried to understand it.

'If it sold for $6 million, it must be art!'
People often think monetary value and artistic value are the same thing. Some works of art command huge prices for a good reason, mainly that only one exists. But there is also a global commercial art industry that has more to do with making money than artistic merit – and that's for people with more money than (artistic) sense.

'Modern art –
I could do that!
Yeah, but you didn't.'
Craig Damrauer

'That's not art, it's too ugly.'
Newsflash: art doesn't have to be beautiful. OK, once upon a time, art was valued for its beauty. Think of a portrait of Elizabeth I: the painter would always show her off to her best advantage for fear of getting his head cut off. But those days are gone. Art should make you think, whether it's pretty or not.

Abstract Expressionism
Letting it All Out

COOL MOVEMENTS

The aim of abstract art is not to represent people or objects directly, but to deal with form, colour and the senses. **Kandinsky** saw abstraction as a way to liberate art. There were many types of abstract styles throughout the 20th century and a huge amount of experimentation and expression.

Artifacts
Important Expressionists of the era (1946–1966) were Wassily Kandinsky, Piet Mondrian, Willem de Kooning, Jackson Pollock, Lee Krasner, Mark Rothko and Franz Kline.

Splash it All Over

In contrast with the Impressionists, who sought to capture the atmospheric effects of light in nature, the Expressionists wanted to convey their feelings. This was a new thing in art and meant that painting no longer had to document the external world, but could show the internal workings of the mind.

Abstract Expressionism, the act of making personal emotions visible through paint and colour, became a definable movement after the Second World War, when American artists from the New York School took up this aggressive and intense style. The late 1940s were an uncertain time: people felt wary of the looming Cold War. The radical and wild new art of abstract impression seemed to reflect the uneasy mood of the moment.

Action Speaks Louder than Words

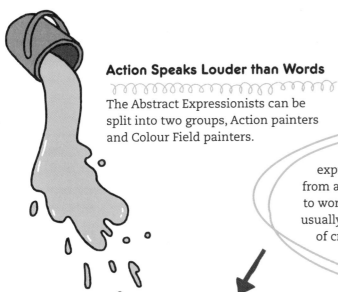

The Abstract Expressionists can be split into two groups, Action painters and Colour Field painters.

Action painting is angry, wild, unplanned expression – flinging paint across a canvas, dripping it from a can, sweeping and smearing it around. The idea was to work unthinkingly, without intention or plan. The result, usually a messy riot of colour, is less important than the act of creating it. Jackson Pollock is the best-known Action painter, closely followed by de Kooning and Franz Kline.

Colour Field painters took a calmer, less angry approach to the same sorts of ideas, painting large areas of colour onto huge canvases. The reflective, meditative work felt like an antidote to the turmoil of the world just after the Second World War.

The impact of Abstract Expressionism caused a geographical shift in the art world. New York finally took the crown from Paris as the most important city in the world for contemporary art.

The Big Picture

One: Number 1 Jackson Pollock

Jackson Pollock's 'drip' painting technique involved pinning a large canvas to the floor, then splashing, dripping, flicking and pouring paint over it with sticks and brushes. Don't try it at home, unless you want to get really messy.

Pollock the Shaman

Pollock would move over the canvas with a paint can and brush as if performing a tribal dance; he chose this method to avoid any pictorial representation. Pollock was interested in primitive art, myths and spiritual rituals. He saw himself as a channel through which the creation of art flowed, saying 'while I am painting I am not aware of what I am doing. The painting has a life of its own; I try to let it come through'.

Pollock captured the imagination of many people and became famous and wealthy very quickly. Pollock was also a troubled man, who struggled with alcohol addiction throughout his life. He died aged 44, when he crashed his car after a bout of drinking.

Drop by drop!

'A good seventy years more and I think I'll make a good artist – **being an artist is life itself** – living it I mean.'
Jackson Pollock

In 2006, one of Pollock's 1948 paintings became the most expensive work of art in history when a buyer paid $140 million for it. It's since been overtaken, however, by Paul Cézanne's *The Card Players*.

One: Number 1 is one of Pollock's biggest paintings, and was made very quickly in the summer of 1950.

Pollock's wild outpourings were seen as a response to the issues of the 1950s, such as aeroplanes, radios and fear of the atom bomb.

Originality
Are There Any New Ideas?

No matter how original you think you may be, everything you have ever thought of has already been done. But don't worry – in art that doesn't matter. It's how YOU do it that makes it different.

Standing on the Shoulders of Giants

If you are setting out to be an artist, designer or any sort of creative person, you need to be realistic about your own ideas and originality. Essentially, you won't have any new ones. But don't be downhearted about it – good artists know that all creative work builds on what has gone before.

So what's the point in bothering? Well, as an artist you can still share your ability and ideas. And timing counts – you may be able to express an idea more effectively than anyone ever has before. Or you may be able to combine techniques in a way that hasn't been possible until now. So while the essence of what you've made may not be 'original', your take on things is definitely worth exploring.

'Good artists copy, great artists steal.'

Pablo Picasso

> **Who do you think is a true art original?**

A Homage to Homage

If nothing is original and all artists are doing is reproducing what has gone before, is that not just theft? That depends on the intention of the artist. If they take an idea and present it as their own, then that is theft, but if they take inspiration and represent it in a well-thought-out way, then it could be regarded as a clever homage. Ultimately, you have to produce the piece of art that you want to make.

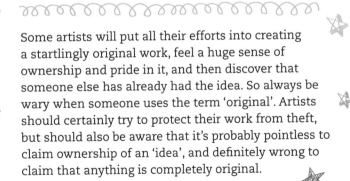

> **That was my idea!**

It's All Been Done Before

Some artists will put all their efforts into creating a startlingly original work, feel a huge sense of ownership and pride in it, and then discover that someone else has already had the idea. So always be wary when someone uses the term 'original'. Artists should certainly try to protect their work from theft, but should also be aware that it's probably pointless to claim ownership of an 'idea', and definitely wrong to claim that anything is completely original.

Pop Art
Famous for More Than 15 Minutes

Pop Art was a brash and brightly coloured art movement that exploded into America in the late 1950s.

Pop Goes America

The 1950s was a time of rapid cultural change: the Second World War was over and business was booming. People found themselves in a land of plenty, with the boom in the economy creating jobs, incomes, spending sprees and, of course, mass production and advertising. Pop Art was the logical response to all this activity; a satirical mirror. Roy Lichtenstein meticulously replicated the printing technique of the period, in which images were made up of sequences of dots, except Lichtenstein carefully hand-painted each one. Andy Warhol used the most popular media images and consumer products he could think of, Claes Oldenburg made huge floppy models of burgers and Jasper Johns famously painted a copy of the American flag.

Artifacts

The predominant colours used by Pop Art artists are yellow, red and blue. In contrast to other art movements, Pop Art's colours don't reflect the artists' inner reflection of the world, they refer to the brashness of popular culture.

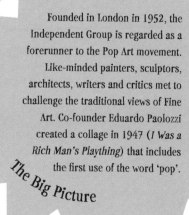

Founded in London in 1952, the Independent Group is regarded as a forerunner to the Pop Art movement. Like-minded painters, sculptors, architects, writers and critics met to challenge the traditional views of Fine Art. Co-founder Eduardo Paolozzi created a collage in 1947 (*I Was a Rich Man's Plaything*) that includes the first use of the word 'pop'.

The Big Picture

not art   not art   not art

ART

Food for Thought

Pop Art pops up as collages, objects or sculptures, or often as carefully painted oils on canvas. Pop Art brought low culture into the realm of high art, parodying mass production and the kitsch aesthetic of advertising.

Some critics say Pop isn't 'proper' art, but it was a movement that had a lot to say, and a new way of saying it. Pop artists were trying to find ways to make people pause and reflect. Was the commercial culture of consumerism and the American Dream really going to provide everything society needed?

Andy Warhol
The King of Pop Art

In a career that spanned almost 40 years, Andy Warhol was a visionary creative force of the 20th century whose work is still parodied, imitated and reproduced to this day.

A Pop Art Icon

Andy Warhol was a sickly child and spent a lot of time in bed. He used that time mainly to draw, and to gaze at his collection of film-star photographs.

He began his career as a commercial artist in New York, creating images for magazines, advertisements and record covers. During the 1950s he first began exhibiting his work in New York and later also in Los Angeles.

In 1964, Warhol converted a New York warehouse into an art studio-cum-general hangout called The Factory, where he mass-produced his art and made films. It soon became a party hotspot that attracted the hippest and wealthiest celebrities in town.

Warhol continued to work, at a slower pace, during the 1970s and 1980s, but died suddenly in 1987 after a routine operation.

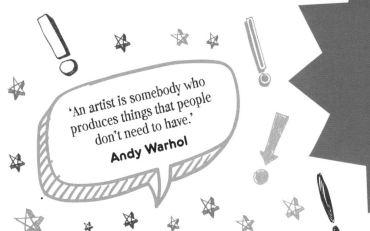

'An artist is somebody who produces things that people don't need to have.'

Andy Warhol

Modern-day Still Life

Warhol's great innovation was the way he made art from the culture that surrounded him. He appropriated photographs from mass media and enlarged them, he took images from advertising, he reproduced bank notes and he used objects from the daily life of the American consumer. He then used repetition of these mundane items to draw attention to consumer culture, mass production, and the dehumanizing effect he felt automation was having on society.

His work intentionally refuted any claims art had to originality: he produced silk-screen prints of Campbell's soup cans and exhibited them in rows just like on a supermarket shelf. He's perhaps most famous for his repetitive series of celebrity portraits in garish colours. These typified the contradictory nature of his work: was he mocking the celebrities, or endorsing them? Was he using their fame to leverage his own? Either way, celebrities and socialites were queuing up for portraits from him.

Fashion and Art

Fashion and art make an odd couple: they are always flirting with each other, meeting up, hanging out for a while, falling out and getting back together again. They have had a long relationship and like many couples, when it comes to money, they have made some terrible choices!

'Art produces ugly things which frequently become more beautiful with time. Fashion produces beautiful things which always become ugly with time.'
Jean Cocteau

60s dress influenced by Mondrian

Keeping it Real?

Fashion tries to justify the commerce at its heart by associating itself with authenticity. It looks for authenticity anywhere it can find it, from youth culture on council estates to nightclubs and art galleries: anywhere where a new sound or style is happening. Fashion will then appropriate the scene, either by stealing it or buying it, and launch a new range.

Art-pop icon Lady Gaga's meat dress

Don't Forget Your Handbag

The association of fashion with art has a strong effect. Take luxury brand Louis Vuitton's ongoing collaborations with contemporary artists. An outrageously overpriced handbag is simply a status symbol that shows other people that you have the money to buy one. But when Louis Vuitton pays an artist to endorse and re-style the bag with multi-coloured patterns, as they have with Japanese artists such as Takashi Murakami or Yayoi Kusama, then something extra happens. Owning one of these artist-designed bags not only suggests that you have the money, but you also have a degree of intelligence, sophistication and taste. Of all the luxury possessions, art is number one.

This Artwork is Sponsored by...

The consumer is only one side of the affair: they hand over the money to make the relationship work. For centuries creative souls like artists and writers have enjoyed financial support from all sorts of benefactors and sponsors. The wealthy supported artists for a number of reasons: sometimes it was genuine philanthropy, but equally it could also be to ensure a place at the best tables, or for possible salvation in Heaven.

The relationship between artist and benefactor is often difficult: usually the benefactor wants something in return for his or her investment, or keeps asking for more until the line between culture and commerce is lost. This confusion is exemplified by Damien Hirst and the Young British Artists (see page 104).

Mark Rothko
The Emotional
Expressionist

COOL ARTISTS

One of the most famous post-war American artists, Mark Rothko rejected the label of Abstract Expressionism and insisted that his paintings represented emotions themselves, often never naming or framing his own works.

Rothko Checklist – How Much do you Know?

To celebrate Rothko's simplistic vision, let's pay homage by ticking off what we know about him:

☐ Mark Rothko was born in Latvia, then in 1913 emigrated to New York with his family.

☐ Between 1921 and 1923, Rothko attended Yale University. He visited museums and galleries after class, where he discovered the work of Henri Matisse and Joan Miró. He became heavily preoccupied with Matisse's *Red Studio* painting, which he visited and studied every day for several months; later, he claimed that *Red Studio* was the basis for all his abstract paintings.

☐ After Yale, Rothko moved to New York City and worked as a teacher.

☐ In 1933 his work was exhibited at the Museum of Art in Portland and the Contemporary Arts Gallery in New York.

☐ During the 1940s Rothko became part of the loose group of Abstract Expressionists, with other artists including Jackson Pollock, Willem de Kooning and Adolph Gottlieb.

☐ Rothko spent his career attempting to 'bring joy and alleviate sadness in others,' but was unable to manage it himself.

'You are entirely lost in colour, you are completely suffused by it, as if it were music.'

In 1958 Rothko was commissioned to paint a series of murals to decorate the walls of the Four Seasons restaurant in the Seagram building in New York, and over a period of three months he completed 40 paintings in red and brown. He even altered the horizontal format of his paintings to complement the restaurant's vertical features. However, Rothko disliked the atmosphere of the restaurant and refused to continue the project. On the morning his body was discovered, one series of the Seagram murals arrived in London to be exhibited at the Tate Gallery. They now occupy a dramatic room of their own at Tate Modern.

Colour Therapy

Rothko painted blurred and formless shapes that looked like weightless clouds. A series of pictures he called 'multiforms' were imposing: 3m (10ft) high canvases, on which he carefully painted colour in thin layers. His aim was to give the viewer the impression they were looking inside the colour itself. His paintings are notorious for their effect; people become absorbed by them, just as Rothko had by Matisse, and they cause an emotional response.

'I'm only interested in expressing basic human emotions – tragedy, ecstasy, doom, and so on.'

Jean-Michel Basquiat
Cultural Hero

The first person to bring street art into the mainstream, Basquiat's unique combination of social commentary, African art and his own personal symbolism brought him fame at a young age.

American Graffiti

When Basquiat was seven years old he was run over by a car. He was in hospital for a month, where he studied the medical textbook *Gray's Anatomy* to pass the time – a book that would be a big influence.

Basquiat started out as a graffiti artist in New York in the late 1970s and progressed onto large-scale canvases when he was a teenager. He was politically and socially aware, and his work attacked oppression and racism. He began showing work in New York galleries in 1980, aged 19, and was noticed by the influential *Artforum* magazine, which ran a big feature on his work and propelled him from the clandestine world of graffiti artists into the more traditional art world.

In 1983 he became friends with Andy Warhol, who acted as a mentor and exhibition organiser for the 23-year-old Basquiat. For a few short years Basquiat was the toast of the New York art scene, adored by collectors and critics alike, but when Andy Warhol died suddenly in 1987, Basquiat's personal life went into freefall, and he died of a heroin overdose the following year, aged just 27.

'Believe it or not, I can actually draw'.

No one seems entirely sure how to pronounce 'Basquiat'. In French, the letter 't' would be silent, so the name would be pronounced 'Bahz-keya', or 'Bahz-kway'. However, the characters in the film of Basquiat's life (Basquiat, 1996) pronounced it 'Bahz-key-ot'. According to some old recordings, Basquiat himself uses the pronunciation 'Bahz-key-aht'.

The Big Picture

Definitely not SAMO

Basquiat and his friend Al Diaz created a graffiti 'character' called SAMO, who pledged 'an end to mindwash religion, nowhere politics, and bogus philosophy.' The SAMO tag could be spotted all over downtown Manhattan between 1977 and 1981. When Diaz and Basquiat fell out in 1981, 'SAMO© IS DEAD' started appearing on buildings, presumably put there by Basquiat.

Minimalism

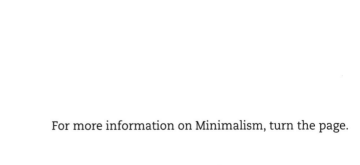

For more information on Minimalism, turn the page.

Minimalism:
Back to Basics

Most new art movements are a reaction to the ones that went before. A good example is the extreme art of Minimalism, which rose up against the dominant, rather messier trend of Abstract Expressionism.

Artifacts

Popular Minimalists of the 1960s and 1970s were Donald Judd, Agnes Martin, Frank Stella, Anne Truitt, Robert Morris, Dan Flavin, Carl Andre, Sol LeWitt, Jo Baer, Robert Mangold and John McCracken.

Enjoy the Silence

Minimalism is a belief in purity and form. Minimalist artists believed that the only way to free art from the messy, decorative past is to strip away every possible adornment. Minimalism reversed the trend of Abstract Expressionism by rejecting all emotional subjectivity (and slopped-about paint) and replacing it with a carefully considered, spartan, mathematical approach. They thought art should be made from modern materials such as bricks, aluminium and fluorescent lights.

Donald Judd and his contemporaries, Frank Stella, Carl Andre and Sol LeWitt, stripped art back to extraordinary levels of bareness. Most of the work they created was three-dimensional, using geometric shapes. Judd stopped giving his work titles, Andre stopped putting his work on plinths or display stands. Anything that could be removed was, including the implied presence of the artists themselves.

Conceptual Art

Sol LeWitt removed himself from his artwork entirely by getting other people to make it for him. He went further by not even being there during the creation of the work. He would write down what he wanted made in a simple note, and pass it on. And he didn't really care if the work turned out to look wildly different from what he asked for – what mattered to him was the handwritten note itself, the concept. The idea was superior to the outcome. With LeWitt, we arrive at Conceptual Art.

A Pile of Old...?

In 1972 Carl Andre's *Equivalent VIII* was purchased by the Tate Gallery in London. This neat arrangement of bricks may not have been everybody's idea of art, but it certainly got people into the gallery – not such a mad purchase as the British press tried to make out, then.

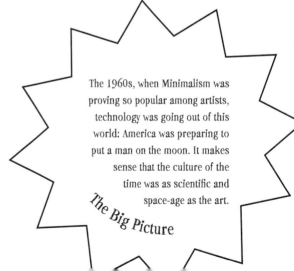

The 1960s, when Minimalism was proving so popular among artists, technology was going out of this world: America was preparing to put a man on the moon. It makes sense that the culture of the time was as scientific and space-age as the art.

The Big Picture

COOL
WORKS
OF ART #8

Untitled
(I Shop Therefore I Am)
Barbara Kruger

In the 1980s Barbara Kruger created a powerful series of work that commented on the state of society. Kruger's characteristic style combined black-and-white photographic images with pithy slogans in white on red text.

Untitled

Taken at face value, the meaning of this piece of work seems obvious: shopping gives us a sense of who we are. The words are a reworking of the famous statement made by philosopher René Descartes: 'I think, therefore I am', which was the argument he used to prove that he existed.

Remixing Descartes gives Kruger's comment extra impact: the implication being that people don't think any more, they just shop. We once looked to great thinkers for ideas about our sense of self, but we now rely on commercial products. I think we can safely say that this is even truer now than it was in 1987.

Artifacts

Kruger was famous for her use of pronouns (I, you, your, we...), as well as using only two fonts: Futura Bold Oblique or Helvetica Ultra Condensed.

What Happened Next?

In the early 2000s something unexpected happened. An advertising agency called Mother, well known for its ability to create campaigns that appealed to a culturally savvy audience, saw Kruger's art and thought it would work brilliantly for an advertising campaign for a famous London department store. They contacted Kruger, who, rather unexpectedly, agreed to collaborate – for a large fee.

So an artwork that originally made a statement against consumerism was being used to sell products. Argh! Kruger justified this by saying that it was much better to have her slogan seen by thousands of different people on the high street, than for it to be stuck in a gallery. She made public art, so this odd marriage of culture and commerce was legitimate. Do you think she was right?

Kruger's other major works include the phrases 'Your Body is a Battleground', 'Your Comfort is my Silence' and 'You Invest in the Divinity of this Masterpiece'

The Big Picture

Performance Art
All The World's A Stage

Performance art has roots in the early 20th century. People were trying to come to terms with the horrors of the First World War, and reacted with shock and awe tactics of their own. Art as performance has evolved ever since.

Happenings Galore

In early 20th-century Vienna, and at the Cabaret Voltaire in Zurich, the Dadaists launched into frantic dance performances and garbled poetry. The French Surrealists focused on the absurd, while the Italian Futurists held banquets of inedible food, all in the name of art. After the Second World War the term 'happening' – meaning a performance, event, or situation with a non-linear storyline and the active participation of the audience – started to appear more and more in connection with a range of art events, including elements of theatre, dance, sculpture, music and poetry. Art was no longer just for galleries.

Artifacts

Yoko Ono's first conceptual art exhibit included the piece 'Hammer A Nail', in which people hammered a nail into a wooden block, creating a different piece of art with each new nail.

Becoming Part of the Art

In Performance Art there is a sense of liberation: the moment only happens once, you have to be there to experience it, and it isn't something that can be kept or sold. Performance artists also have a variety of new tricks at their disposal. Yves Klein, for example, covered nude models in blue paint and rolled them across canvases in pursuit of pure and true art, while the Blue Man Group have achieved worldwide success for becoming part of their own art.

Mad as a March Hare

Joseph Beuys took things a step further in 1965. His idea was to create rumours, myths and stories and to be remembered as the first to carry them out. So, who has covered themselves in honey, worn one shoe made of felt and another made of iron, and then walked around an art gallery explaining each of the pictures on the walls to a dead hare? Yep, it was Joseph Beuys.

Living Sculptures

Gilbert & George are two of Britain's most eccentric – and beloved – performance artists. A collaborative duo, the pair regard themselves as living sculptures, refusing to untangle their art from their own everyday lives, and insisting that absolutely everything they do is art. In 1986, Gilbert & George won the Turner prize, the first artists to win with pieces that were not paintings.

Gilbert & George

Ai Weiwei
China's Controversial Master

Emerging as one of China's most groundbreaking (and urn-breaking) artists, Ai Weiwei is driven by his fierce beliefs to blur the boundaries between art and politics and his desire to make artistic and social statements with every one of his contemporary pieces. Born in Beijing in 1957, Weiwei is currently China's most famous living artist (and architect, blogger, curator, designer, activist and poet).

Artifacts

One of Wewei's most infamous pieces is his 'Dropping A Han Dynasty Urn, 1995' triptych. The artist was photographed letting go of an ancient, and irreplaceable, ceramic artefact that smashed at his feet. This piece demonstrated his questioning attitude towards cultural values and the destruction of social history.

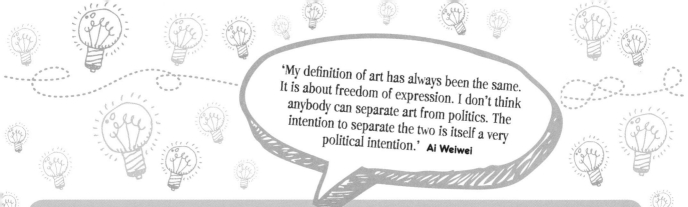

'My definition of art has always been the same. It is about freedom of expression. I don't think anybody can separate art from politics. The intention to separate the two is itself a very political intention.' **Ai Weiwei**

What do we know about Weiwei? Here's a checklist

❑ Ai Weiwei was the artistic consultant for the Beijing National Stadium (known as the 'Bird's Nest'), built for the Olympics in 2008.

❑ His 'Sunflower Seeds' exhibit at Tate Modern, London in 2010 consisted of 100 million ceramic 'seeds' spread across the floor in a huge carpet. The seeds had been individually hand-painted in China by a team of over 1,600 artisans. The work was a statement about mass production, Chinese industry and consumerism.

❑ Since the beginning of his career Weiwei has always spoken out against the Chinese regime. While he produces beautiful and affecting large-scale artworks, he also arranges a great deal of activism and protest.

❑ Much of his art is a response to restrictions, limitations and being marginalised. Although he cannot leave Beijing, he still continues to create art and to arrange exhibitions around the world.

❑ Ai's criticism of the Chinese government was never going to be allowed to go unchecked. Since 2008 he has been arrested, beaten by police, had his studio demolished by authorities and been illegally detained for two months in terrible conditions.

Prints of Thieves

Art theft always makes great headlines, as well as exciting plots in blockbuster movies. While sadly only a small proportion of stolen art is ever recovered, you can't help but be amazed by the audacity and arrogance of art thieves. So, ladies and gentleman, I give you the three greatest art robberies of the past century...

A Police Raid With a Difference

The biggest art theft in American history took place at the Isabella Stewart Gardner Museum in Boston in March 1990, where artworks with an estimated value of $300 million were successfully seized by two thieves disguised as police officers. The 13 pieces stolen included paintings by Degas, Manet, Vermeer and Rembrandt. The case is still unsolved and a reward of $5 million is on offer for the safe return of the paintings. To make matters even worse for the small Boston museum, it had failed to arrange an insurance policy.

Stolen Screams

Thieves in Norway seem to have a fetish for Edvard Munch. At the National Gallery of Oslo, Norway, in February 1994, his 1893 masterpiece *The Scream* was stolen. The thieves were caught and the painting was back on display by May.

Ten years later, at Oslo's Munch Museum, another version of *The Scream* was stolen, along with Munch's *Madonna*. They were recovered within two years. And in 1995, three more paintings by Munch were stolen from a hotel in Norway, but these were all recovered the next day.

(the) SCREAM!!

Monet for Nothing

Over in Switzerland in February 2008, two Picasso paintings worth around £2 million were stolen from an exhibition in the town of Pfäffikon. Then, just four days later, and a short distance away in Zurich, three masked men waving guns raided the Emil Buehrle Collection just before closing time. They stole four works by Cézanne, Degas, Monet and van Gogh, valued at around £84 million. Two weeks later, the Monet and the van Gogh were found in a car park in Zurich and in 2012 the Cézanne was recovered in Serbia. The Degas painting is still missing.

Outsider Art
Working From the Outside In

Outsider art is a term used to describe artists who aren't formally trained in art, don't belong to any artistic group and exist on the fringes of society. Outsider artists may have difficulty communicating their thoughts and feelings, so they choose art as a medium of self-expression.

Art of the Insane

The term 'outsider art' was first used in 1972 by the British art critic Roger Cardinal. An equivalent term in French, formulated by the painter Jean Dubuffet in the 1940s, is *Art Brut*, meaning 'rough art' or 'raw art'.

Outsider artists often don't set out to make art – they are simply using any materials they have at their disposal, often compulsively, to build, paint, sculpt and illustrate their own personal thoughts and obsessions.

It's only later, when other people (including art dealers) get involved, that it becomes seen as art.

Many critics are baffled by outsider art, but it is now an established and influential field within contemporary art, and has its share of collectors. Outsider art is fascinating as it shows us a unique, alternative vision of the world, from artists who aren't artists. Seeing the universe through the eyes of another person is a very powerful experience.

Artifacts

Adolf Wölfli was one of the most renowned outsider artists; he spent most of his adult life in an insane asylum, and made thousands of complex drawings of imaginary adventures.

Outsider art began in 19th century European psychiatric hospitals. Doctors collected the drawings of mental patients (not as medical evidence but as art) and published books of their work, granting their paintings a wider audience. The most influential of these was *A Mental Patient As Artist*, a book which provided the first monograph of an outsider artist, Adolf Wölfli.

The Big Picture

Method in the Madness

Many famous 'Outsiders' are eccentric characters, while others have a disability such as autism or Down's Syndrome. Henry Darger was a recluse; Howard Finster was a preacher who painted slogans and sermons; Bill Traylor was an ex-slave; Martin Ramirez was a Mexican-born psychiatric patient; and Madge Gill believed she had a spiritual guide that made her draw young women's faces surrounded by complex geometric patterns.

'There is always some reason in madness'
Friedrich Nietzsche

The Value of Art

Here's a picture. What do you think about it? Do you like it? Let me tell you something about it...

This painting is an Abstract Expressionist piece painted by Joel Weldon Kees in New York in 1968, which sold at Christie's auction house in London in 2009 for £4.5 million.

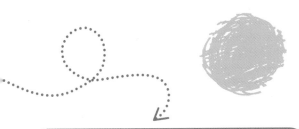

Actually, that's a lie. This painting was made by a three-year-old girl at nursery school. Her mum has it taped to the wall of her office to remind her of her daughter while she's at work.

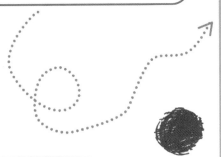

'Making money is art and working is art, and good business is the best art.'
Andy Warhol

Background Becomes Foreground

Fooled you! OK, neither of these 'facts' is true – the picture was knocked up by our illustrator. But did you think differently about the picture while reading each of the two descriptions? When you thought it was an expensive work of art, could you see how the colours are deliberately chosen? Could you see structure in the picture, an intention? Does the idea that it is worth £4.5 million make you like it more than you would otherwise have done?

When you thought it was a child's painting, could you suddenly see the sloppy and random way the colours were applied? Does it seem unplanned, and only of personal value to the 'artist's' mother, rather than as a work of art?

It's really difficult to stop information about the artist affecting how you 'see' a painting. With no fixed rules about what constitutes a work of art, we are often left to make our own judgements, so the tiniest piece of background information can easily sway our opinion.

Damien Hirst
The Entrepreneurial Artist

COOL ARTISTS

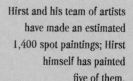

Artifacts
Damien Hirst is the world's wealthiest living artist, worth over £200 million.

Throughout the late 1980s and 1990s, Hirst presented a series of new concepts to the art world, and has significantly changed perceptions of art – whether we agree with him or not.

Taste of His Own Medicine – Let's Dissect Hirst!

❑ Hirst grew up in Leeds and received an E in A-level art, but still managed to study at Goldsmiths College, London.

❑ While studying he met advertising mogul Charles Saatchi, who agreed to fund his work.

❑ Hirst is known for dunking sharks, cows and sheep into formaldehyde, artworks made from butterflies (both alive and dead), and his extensive series of spin and spot paintings as well as diamond-encrusted skull.

❑ Hirst shares the view of many 20th-century artists that the idea is more important than the work and that the artist's 'hand' is no longer important.

Hirst and his team of artists have made an estimated 1,400 spot paintings; Hirst himself has painted five of them.

The Big Picture

'It's amazing what you can do with an E in A-level art, a twisted imagination and a chainsaw.'

The Business of Art

Hirst has always been preoccupied with the idea of money-making and self-promotion. The tiger shark he placed in a glass tank of formaldehyde (*The Impossibility of Death in the Mind of Someone Living*) sold for $12 million. He also had a human skull encrusted with millions of pounds' worth of diamonds (*For The Love Of God*), then sold it as a work of art for twice its value. No one else could do this kind of thing, but does this make Hirst an artist or a unique racketeer?

Creating the Shark

Hirst's *Tiger Shark* is a icon of modern art. But the shark you see now in galleries is not the original one when the work first appeared in 1991. That shark decayed in the formaldehyde solution. Before the piece was sold, Hirst replaced the shark with a new one, begging the question – is it the same piece of art? Hirst acknowledged this: 'Artists and conservators have different opinions about what's important: the original artwork or the original intention. I come from a conceptual art background, so I think it should be the intention. It's the same piece. But the jury will be out for a long time to come.' What do you think?

Banksy
Global Street Artist

Banksy became known in the late 1990s for his large-scale, satirical stencil paintings on walls and bridges around his Bristol hometown, and then Hackney and Shoreditch in London. His sarcastic, anti-establishment wordplay and subverted artworks appeared on walls around the UK and then the world.

Can You Believe It?

Banksy began as a fairly typical graffiti artist in Bristol, but broke away from the purist graffiti scene by using stencils. Graffiti-art purists pride themselves on free-hand spray painting and 'can-control'; preparing cut-out stencils is cheating and against the rules, but Banksy didn't care. Many graffiti artists regarded him as a cheat and a sell-out, but before long they wished they'd thought of it first.

A tactical self-promoter, Banksy strategically placed pieces in areas where he knew fashionable and influential young people would see and talk about them. These days, any new work he puts on the street makes headlines all around the world. He has completely outsmarted all the anti-graffiti authorities – if a Banksy piece appears on a wall in your area, it is now council policy not to paint over it, but instead to protect the work as local heritage.

Not all his work is in paint. In 2004 he successfully planted a rat in a glass case into the National History Museum in London. It wasn't spotted for several hours, despite the fact that it was wearing sunglasses!

HAVE YOU SEEN THIS MAN?

The Stencil is King!

Graffiti art took off as a subcultural activity in the UK in the late 1980s, and it took the police about ten years to contain it. By the late 1990s there was CCTV everywhere, improved security at train stations, anti-graffiti police teams and heavier fines and convictions, which seriously curtailed the graffiti scene. The only successful way to put work up in the street was to be secretive and extremely quick: this is why the stencil was key to Banksy's success – it was so fast.

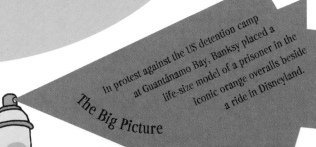

In protest against the US detention camp at Guantánamo Bay, Banksy placed a life-size model of a prisoner in the iconic orange overalls beside a ride in Disneyland.

The Big Picture

IMPORTANT EXHIBITIONS

Salon des Refusés (Exhibition of Rejects)

In 1863, when the French government allowed a group of rejected artists to exhibit their works in an annex to the Paris Salon, they allowed the next generation to show their exciting new paintings to the world.

'The Salon des Refusés is the most decisive institutional development in the progress of modern art.'
Albert Boime

Beautiful Rejects

The judges selecting work for the Paris Salon, the officially approved major exhibition of new artists, were a bit set in their ways. They rejected everything except historical paintings in the traditional style. Unfortunately they were out of step with the times, and the Salon's rejections caused a public outcry. Then Emperor Napoleon III stepped in and demanded that the rejected pictures go on display, resulting in a Salon des Refusés exhibition being set up nearby.

Exhibitors at the Salon des Refusés included progressive talents such as James McNeill Whistler, Paul Cézanne and Camille Pissaro. Most notable, however, was the appearance of Édouard Manet's masterpiece, *Le Dejeuner sur l'Herbe*. By depicting a nude woman in a modern-day setting, Manet insulted the art establishment, who were outraged by his lack of dignity and decorum, but that didn't stop the public from crowding in.

Damien Hirst's Freeze

In July 1988, a group of sixteen art students from Goldsmiths College in London, now known as the Young British Artists, or YBAs for short, organised this exhibition in London's Docklands called Freeze.

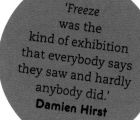

Eventful Art Events

Damien Hirst was the orchestrator of the exhibition, rounding up all his contacts and college mates to make it happen. He deliberately set up the exhibition space to mimic Charles Saatchi's gallery in North London, possibly to attract Saatchi's attention. The show featured his fellow students, many of whom have since gone on to become notable artists, including Sarah Lucas, Gary Hume, Fiona Rae, Michael Landy and Mat Collishaw.

Hirst's bait worked. Charles Saatchi was lured into attending and he bought one of Collishaw's pieces. The director of the Tate Gallery visited, as did the Exhibitions Secretary of the Royal Academy, along with several journalists and art critics. A new wave of British artists was born. Ten years later, many of the artists featured in another show called *Sensation* at the Royal Academy. The controversy caused by the content of the exhibition cemented the fame and market value of the artists on show.

A–Z of Art

Avant-Garde French for 'advance guard', referring to people pushing boundaries with ideas ahead of their time.

Biennale Italian word used to describe an international art exhibition that happens every two years (biennially).

Contemporary art Art by artists who are still alive. Contemporary art has no connection to any particular group, style or technique, it is simply art from the present day.

Curator Person in charge of organising an art exhibition. Curators spend years studying art and picking up all the clever jargon to describe it (see Praxis, below).

De Stijl Art movement founded in the Netherlands during the First World War. The artists and architects involved sought to create a universal language using only horizontal and vertical lines and the three primary colours. The name comes from the title of a Dutch magazine run by Piet Mondrian called *The Style*.

Ephemera Handwritten notes, bus tickets, diaries, rough sketches, old photographs – any random items not meant to be kept that are either turned into art pieces or displayed in exhibitions to give context to an artist.

Fauvism French for 'wild beasts', Fauvism is a style of painting from the early 20th century associated with

Henri Matisse. The style emphasised bold colours and heavy brushstrokes over realism.

Gouache Name given to opaque watercolour paint, and also to a painting produced with it.

Happening Unscripted, spontaneous performance by an artist or collective, often improvised in a public space.

Iconoclasm Act of attacking established beliefs, institutions or artworks. An artist can be an iconoclast if she makes a work that insults the state. If the state then destroys the work, that would also be an act of iconoclasm.

Juxtaposition Technique of placing colours or subjects close together or alongside each other, causing the viewer to compare and contrast them.

Kinetic sculpture Sculpture that moves. The artwork may be motorised or set into motion by hand or the flow of air or water.

Linocut Technique popularised by Matisse and Picasso for which linoleum is cut, painted, then pressed onto paper. The images tend to be sharper than woodcuts.

Modern art Work from around 1900 to today. The term also refers to the historical period known as Modernism. All art produced after 1900 can be described as 'Modern' as it was created in or after the historical phenomenon called Modernism began.

Motif Where a single element is repeated in a pattern or series. This includes repetition of patterns and shapes in textile art, and also the use of plants, fruit and flowers as symbols.

New media Term to describe a medium of representation in art that is so new, it doesn't have its own name yet. Art produced digitally, such as using augmented reality phone apps, is currently labelled new media.

Ornamentation Decorative adornments and details to add to the beauty of appearance. If one art movement loves adornment, the subsequent one usually hates it, and vice versa.

Praxis Way of saying 'practice' to refer to an artist's work. Often used alongside 'gnosis', which simply means 'knowledge of something'. So when people say 'gnosis and praxis', all they mean is theory and practice, which is basically thinking about stuff and doing stuff.

Quattrocentro Italian term meaning '400' that refers to the 1400s or 15th-century Renaissance period and the artists who revived Greek and Roman art forms.

Rococo 18th-century French decorative style of art and architecture that is highly intricate and ornate. Playful themes presented in pastel colours were a reaction against the more formal Baroque style that preceded it.

Space Fashionable word for an unofficial art gallery. A space can be anywhere, a derelict building, a garden or a car park. A 'pop-up space' is a way of saying 'temporary exhibition'.

Trompe-l'oeil French phrase meaning 'to deceive the eyes'. Used in art to refer to optical illusions, usually when a two-dimensional image appears to be three-dimensional.

Urban Attempt to classify variations of graffiti and street art in a single word. Its use is controversial as it carries with it implications of reference to social class and even race, for example Urban Aboriginal Art.

Vivid A compliment given to a colourful painting. It usually means that it hurts to look at it.

Women artists While the majority of art students are female, and women produce more art than men, they are very much in the minority when it comes to being represented by commercial galleries. Even more curious is the fact that most of the commercial gallery directors, art agents and administrators are women.

X-Ray art Aboriginal style of painting from around 2000 BC in which bone structure and internal organs are externally visible.

YBAs Young British Artists. A group of British-based artists involved in a series of exhibitions of the same name at the Saatchi Gallery in London in the 1990s, including Tracey Emin, Gavin Turk, Sarah Lucas and Damien Hirst.

Zeitgeist handy German word that simply refers to 'our present situation'. Art often addresses our immediate human circumstances.

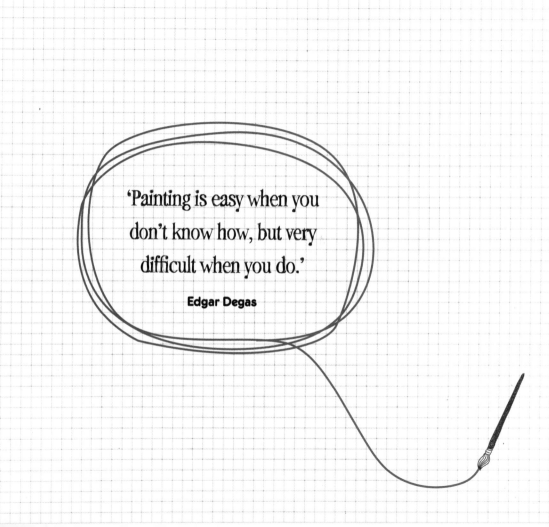

'Painting is easy when you don't know how, but very difficult when you do.'

Edgar Degas